DEVOTIONS for FAMILIES

Building Blocks of Christian Life

BARBARA OWEN WEBB

Cover and Illustrations by Bill Hamilton Associates

JUDSON PRESS, VALLEY FORGE

DEVOTIONS FOR FAMILIES: BUILDING BLOCKS OF CHRISTIAN LIFE

Library of Congress Cataloging in Publication Data

Webb, Barbara Owen.
Devotions for families.

1. Bible. N. T. Ephesians—Meditations. 2. Family—Prayer-books and devotions—English. I. Title.
BS2695.4.W4 227'.5 75-22162
ISBN 0-8170-0680-X

Printed in the U.S.A.

DEVOTIONS for FAMILIES

Building Blocks of Christian Life

Author's Note

Some years ago, when our girls were five and six years old and our active son was only two, we began to have a time of daily devotions. At that time, I would read a devotion similar to the ones in this book, we'd sing a song such as "Jesus Loves Me," and one of the girls would offer a prayer. As the children grew older, they took turns reading and praying, and we closed our devotion time by saying a benediction together. A family devotion time proved to be a unifying and joyful experience for us. The devotions in this book were written that through their use your family might experience this same kind of joy. They are all based on Bible texts from Ephesians with the hope that in future years, when your then-grown children pursue deeper studies of this epistle, their study will be enriched because they will have known this Scripture since childhood.

Blessings!

Barbara Owen Webb

The Illustrations

The line drawings in this book were chosen because they are Christian symbols representing the different themes included here from Ephesians. God, the Father—the hand of God is one of the oldest and main symbols of God, the Father. Jesus Christ—IXΘUS (ichthus) is the Greek word for fish. Each Greek letter in the word is the beginning letter for one of Jesus' titles, Jesus, Christ, Son of God, Savior. The Holy Spirit—the most common symbol for the Holy Spirit is the descending dove. In the first chapter of Mark we read that at Jesus' baptism the Holy Spirit descended "like a dove" (Mark 1:10). Building Together with God's Gifts—to symbolize this section, we use a drawing of the cornerstone of a building. The Christian Fellowship—the vine and branches symbolize the unity of the church, the fellowship of Christians. Care for Others—the cross of suffering symbolizes Christ's suffering and death on the cross. Just as Christ cared enough to die for us, so we should care for others. Use of the Bible—the open Bible reminds us that we should read our Bibles every day. God speaks to us through the Bible. Prayer—the folded hands symbolize prayer. Family Love—to symbolize this section and remind us that we should show our love for other members of our family, we use a line drawing of a family. Worship—the trefoil is the symbol of the Trinity, God as Father, Son, and Holy Spirit. Each symbol is reproduced in a line drawing which can be colored and used as a minibanner. Or they may be used as the basis for creating your own banners. For those who would like variety in their creative activity, a pattern which can be cut out and folded into a block is printed on the reverse side of the line drawing. This pattern is to be cut on the solid lines and folded on the dotted lines. The tabs can then be slipped inside the block, thus holding it together. A reduced version of the Christian symbol is printed on one face of the block. Other pictures may be drawn on the other faces of the blocks; these blocks can then be made into mobiles or pyramids.

For the teachers and students
at Saint Paul's School, Annapolis

How to Greet Others

May God our Father and the Lord Jesus Christ give you grace and peace.
Ephesians 1:2

"Yuk, here comes that new girl," said Ann as she looked out the window. The new girl was walking toward Ann's house. *She sure has on a weird dress and her hair's a mess,* Ann thought. *She even walks funny.*

The new girl knocked on Ann's front door. "Yoo-hoo, Ann," she called. "Would you like to walk to school with me?"

"Uh, no, I'm not ready yet. You better go on," replied Ann.

"Okay, see you at school," she said. The new girl smiled and waved good-bye.

I'll wait until she's around the corner; then I'll start, thought Ann.

How sad for Ann that all she could think about were the things she didn't like about the new girl. There is a happier way to think when we meet someone. Paul, in beginning his Letter to the Ephesians, gives us a clue. His greeting was in a letter, but it applies to greeting someone in person, too. He begins by saying, "May God give you grace and peace." He must have been thinking how much he wanted God's blessing for these people.

We do not need to go up to people and say, "May the Lord give you peace," but this is what we should want for them in our minds. As Jesus meets us each day, he doesn't call to mind all our faults. He forgets them and brings us love and joy. We, too, can bring love and joy to those we meet each day, if we want the best for them.

When we remember this, we will be less apt to look for faults. The next time you meet someone, think a little prayer, "May God bless you," as you say, "Hello." You will be blessed, too.

God Won't Change His Mind

Before the world was made, God had already chosen us to be his in Christ. . . .
Ephesians 1:4

Jimmy stood with his mother in the ice cream store. He looked through the glass case at all the different kinds of ice cream.

"Which kind would you like?" his mother asked. She waited patiently for him to make up his mind.

Jimmy sighed. They all looked so good. "I can't decide whether to get the fudge-nut or the strawberry whiz, or maybe the grape bubble gum flavor," he said.

"I think the fudge-nut looks delicious. That's what I'm going to have," said his mother.

"Eenie, meenie, miney, moe . . ." Jimmy began. At last he chose the strawberry whiz. But then, while Jimmy was licking his cone, he looked at his mother's. Maybe he should have chosen fudge-nut after all, he thought.

Jimmy certainly had a terrible time making up his mind. Even after he made his decision, he wasn't sure it was right. Hasn't that happened to you, too?

Knowing how difficult it can be to choose something makes it seem even more wonderful that God doesn't have that problem. Our Scripture says that even before the world was made, God had chosen us to be his people. Way back then he loved us. He knew that someday each of us would be born into the world, and he wanted us to know him and live happily. And God doesn't change his mind. When we do something wrong, he still loves us. We can be sure because God sent his Son, Jesus, to take away our sins and show us how very much he loves us. Let's give thanks today that a long time ago God chose us for his own.

Faith Brings Peace and Love

May God the Father and the Lord Jesus Christ give peace and love to all the brothers, with faith.
Ephesians 6:23

Mrs. Crandell thought she'd surprise her family with a home-baked cake. She always used cake mixes, but this time she thought she'd make one from scratch. She hummed to herself as she got out the flour, sugar, butter, eggs, and other ingredients. She kept looking back at the cookbook to check the recipe. When the cake was in the oven, she was careful not to open the door too soon or jar the cake. Finally the timer sounded, *ding*. Mrs. Crandell peeked at her cake and then opened the door wide. What had happened? What had gone wrong? The cake was flat, not high and rounded as in the picture. She pulled out the sunken cake and sat down shaking her head. After all that work! She looked back over the recipe. Two words met her eyes for the first time—baking powder. She'd left out the baking powder! Without it, of course the cake wouldn't rise. Mrs. Crandell reached in the cupboard for a mix.

We're talking about some ingredients for Christians today—peace, love, and faith. Faith is like the baking powder that makes the love rise and the peace flow in our hearts. As we listen to God's Word, he builds faith in our hearts. Faith is the confidence that God loved us so much he sent his Son, Jesus, to die for us and rise again. We are sure that Jesus is with us each day in everything we do. Because we are sure of him, we are not afraid to love others who don't care about us. Jesus cares—that's what matters. And we can have peace in the middle of a difficult time because we know Jesus is with us in that difficulty. When Jesus is your Savior, you are always loved and you are never alone.

The Best Thing in Life Is Free

For it is by God's grace that you have been saved, through faith. It is not your own doing, but God's gift.
Ephesians 2:8

Mother reached down to tie two-year-old Timmie's shoelaces. But Timmie pushed her hands away.

"Me do! Me do!" he screamed and twisted the laces around in his fingers, trying to tie a bow.

When Mother tried to button his sweater, the same thing happened. Timmie grabbed the front of his sweater and turned his back to his mother.

"Me do! Me do!" he cried insistently.

Timmie struggled so hard with the buttons that he pulled one off the sweater. He stared at the button in his hand, then threw it on the floor and began to cry very loudly.

It's probably a good thing that two-year-olds want to try to do things for themselves. Otherwise, they might never learn to do many important things. Even older children and adults want to do many things without help from others. But as we get older, we learn what things we *can* do and what things require help from someone else.

There are always some people, though, who still want to do everything themselves. They even want to get to heaven without any help from God. "I'm a good person," they say. "I don't do anything wrong, so I'll go to heaven." But our Bible verse today tells us plainly that we are not saved by what *we* do. Being saved is a free gift from God to those who believe in his Son, Jesus Christ. This is not a time to say, "I'll do it myself," but a time to say, "Thank you, God."

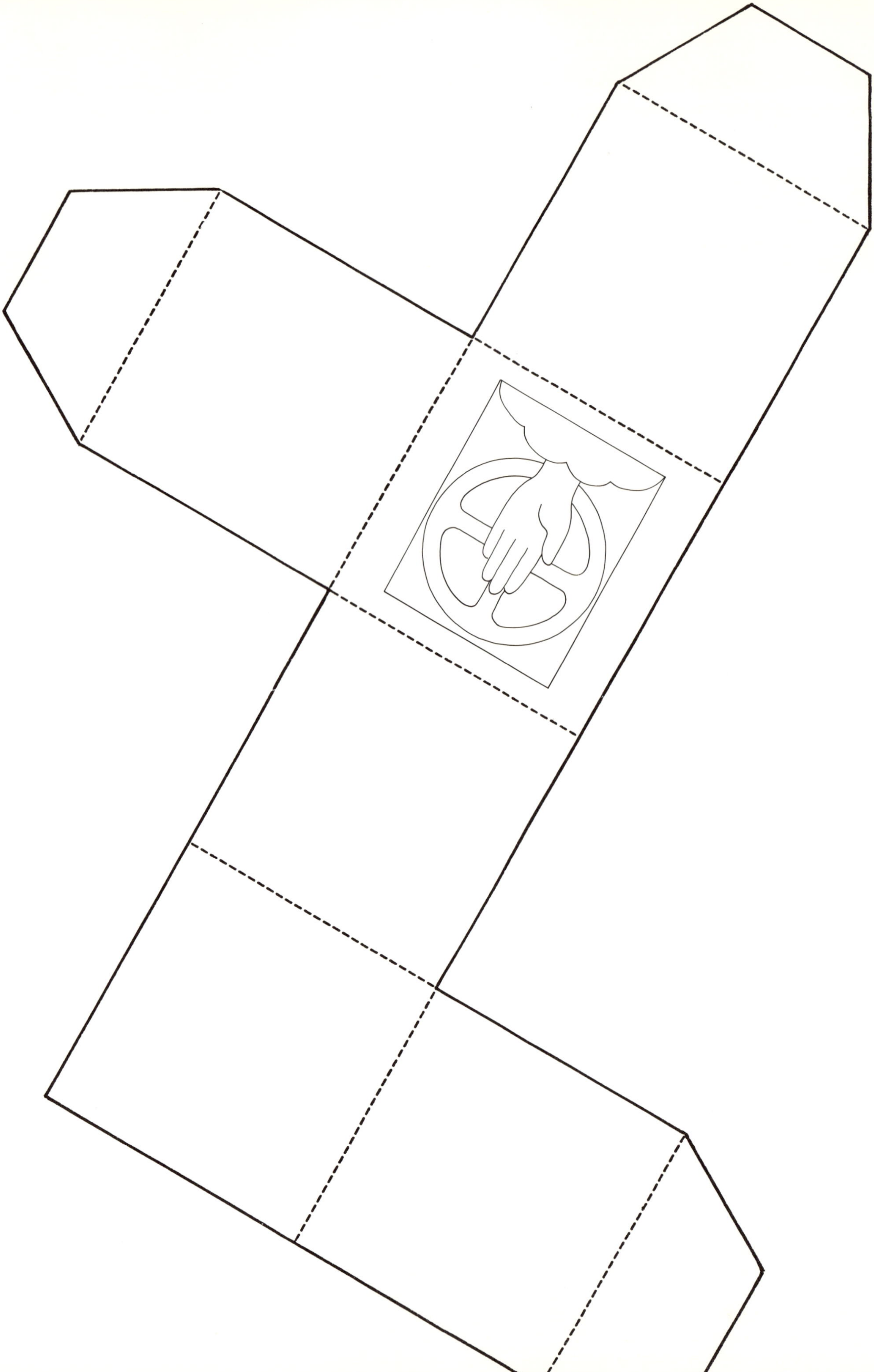

What Is Freedom?

For by the death of Christ we are set free, that is, our sins are forgiven. . . .
Ephesians 1:7

Beverly struggled along the sidewalk, carrying a huge pile of books. Never had the third-grade teacher given so much homework, and Beverly was carrying her library books and extra-credit projects besides. Her arms started to ache. She wished she could put down her load, but the ground was wet from a rainstorm earlier in the day. She would have to keep going until she got home.

A friend's dog came toward her, wagging its tail. The dog expected Beverly to stop and pet him as she usually did. But today she said sternly, "Look out," and went on by.

Beverly's arms ached more and more. All she could think about was how heavy her books were. She didn't want to stop to talk to anyone. When a neighbor lady said, "Hello," Beverly pretended not to hear and hurried on.

When she was almost home, her big brother came by on his bike. "Hey, Bev," he called. "Want to put your stuff in my basket?"

What a relief! She was free from the weight of all those books and walked along happily. She smiled at a little boy riding his tricycle down the sidewalk. She told Mrs. Miller how much she liked her roses. Now she could think about other people instead of the heavy load she was carrying.

It has been said that the heaviest load or burden in the world is that of sin. Sin makes people feel guilty and worried; they can think only about themselves. But God loves us so much that he sent Jesus to take away our burden of sin. When we believe in Jesus as our Savior, God says, "You are forgiven. You are free of the burden of sin." When we remember that we are free of this burden, we don't have to think about ourselves all the time. We can think about other people and find ways to love them as God loves us.

How to Make Up

For Christ himself has brought us peace, by making the Jews and Gentiles one people. . . .
Ephesians 2:14

"There's an imaginary line down the center of this room," Mary said sternly to her sister Jane. "Don't you dare come across it!" She turned and flounced on her bed.

Jane smirked at Mary and stuck her toe over the line. Mary shrieked, jumped off the bed, and shoved Jane. She lost her balance and fell into Jane's side of the room. Jane reached across the line and grabbed Mary's favorite record.

"Give me my record!" gasped Mary.

"Not until you get off my side of the room!" retorted Jane.

"Girls! Girls!" Mother spoke sharply as she appeared in the doorway. She would not listen to the pleas of either girl but made them sit on their beds. Then she read them the Bible verse that we have today, "'For Christ himself has brought us peace, by making the Jews and Gentiles one people.'" She went on to explain, "Long ago, in Old Testament times, only the Jews knew God. But when Jesus came, he made it very clear that he came not only for the Jews, but also for the Gentiles, that is, all the other people in the world. Jesus died for the sins of all people, and anyone who believes in him is part of God's family. This was very amazing to the Jews and Gentiles of long ago. They had been distrusting each other for so long. But when they realized that they both loved Jesus, they learned to love each other, too."

Mary lifted her head and looked at her mother. "I think you mean that since Jane and I both love Jesus, we should love each other, too," she said softly.

"But sometimes . . ." Jane started to protest, but Mother took her hand.

"Sometimes you just get *so* mad," Mother said. "I know. And God knows, too. That's why forgiveness is so wonderful. God will forgive you, and then you can forgive each other. Jesus helps you make up if you've had a quarrel."

Jane handed the record to Mary. "Here's your record," she said.

"Let's erase the imaginary line," said Mary, smiling at last.

Don't Be Afraid of God

In union with him [Christ], and through our faith in him, we have the freedom to enter into God's presence with all confidence. *Ephesians 3:12*

"Wow!" exclaimed Jack. "Your dad sure has a lot of fishing rods!" Jack admired the rods in a rack in Ed's basement. Ed had invited Jack over to go fishing with him.

"You'd probably like that blue spinning rod," said Ed.

"Are you sure your dad won't mind?" asked Jack nervously. "I'd never borrow any of my dad's stuff. He'd get really mad."

"No, Dad won't mind," said Ed. "He's told me I can use any of these rods and share them with my friends. He knows that I know how to take care of them." Ed grinned at his friend. "And you know what? If you get a nice fish, Dad'll be the most excited of all. He's that way."

Jack took the rod in his hands. "Boy, wish my dad was like that," he said as they headed for the river.

In the evening, Jack and Ed came back with a string full of good-sized perch. Ed's dad was home then and looked at the catch. "Nice going, fellows," he said enthusiastically. Later, he told Jack to come back any time.

Perhaps we can understand from this story how happy we can feel with our heavenly Father. When we come to him in prayer, we don't come alone. We come with his Son, Jesus. God loves Jesus and shares all he has with him. God will share his treasures with us, too—treasures such as his love, kindness, gentleness, and joy. We do not have to be afraid of God when Jesus is our friend. God will always be happy to share with us.

A Love Too Big to Imagine

[I pray] . . . that you, together with all God's people, may have the power to understand how broad and long and high and deep is Christ's love. *Ephesians 3:18*

"Gee, Dad," exclaimed Benny, "look at *all* those stars! There must be millions." Benny dug his feet into the sandy beach to steady himself as he looked up at the sky on that clear summer night.

"More than that," said Dad. "The universe is so huge we can't begin to imagine how large it is."

"And what's on the other side of the stars?" asked Benny.

"More stars; stars that are so far away we can't even see them," Dad said.

You've probably looked at the starry sky and marveled at how big the universe is, too. In today's Scripture the apostle Paul is marveling at something else that is very big. He is thinking of the love that Jesus has for people, a love that brought him to the cross to die for our sins, a love that cares about each one of us all the time. Jesus' love is always with you everywhere you go. It always surrounds you just as the stars seem to surround you on a beautiful, clear night. The stars are there for all people to see and enjoy. Jesus' love is for all people, too. Can you imagine loving everybody in the whole world, caring about each person's problems, listening to prayers without losing patience, constantly helping all people and yet never tiring? Jesus does all of this because he loves us.

When we trust in him, he gives us some of this great big love for others. If we feel we are running out of love for someone, we need only ask Jesus for more love to share. His love never runs out.

ΙΧΘΥΣ

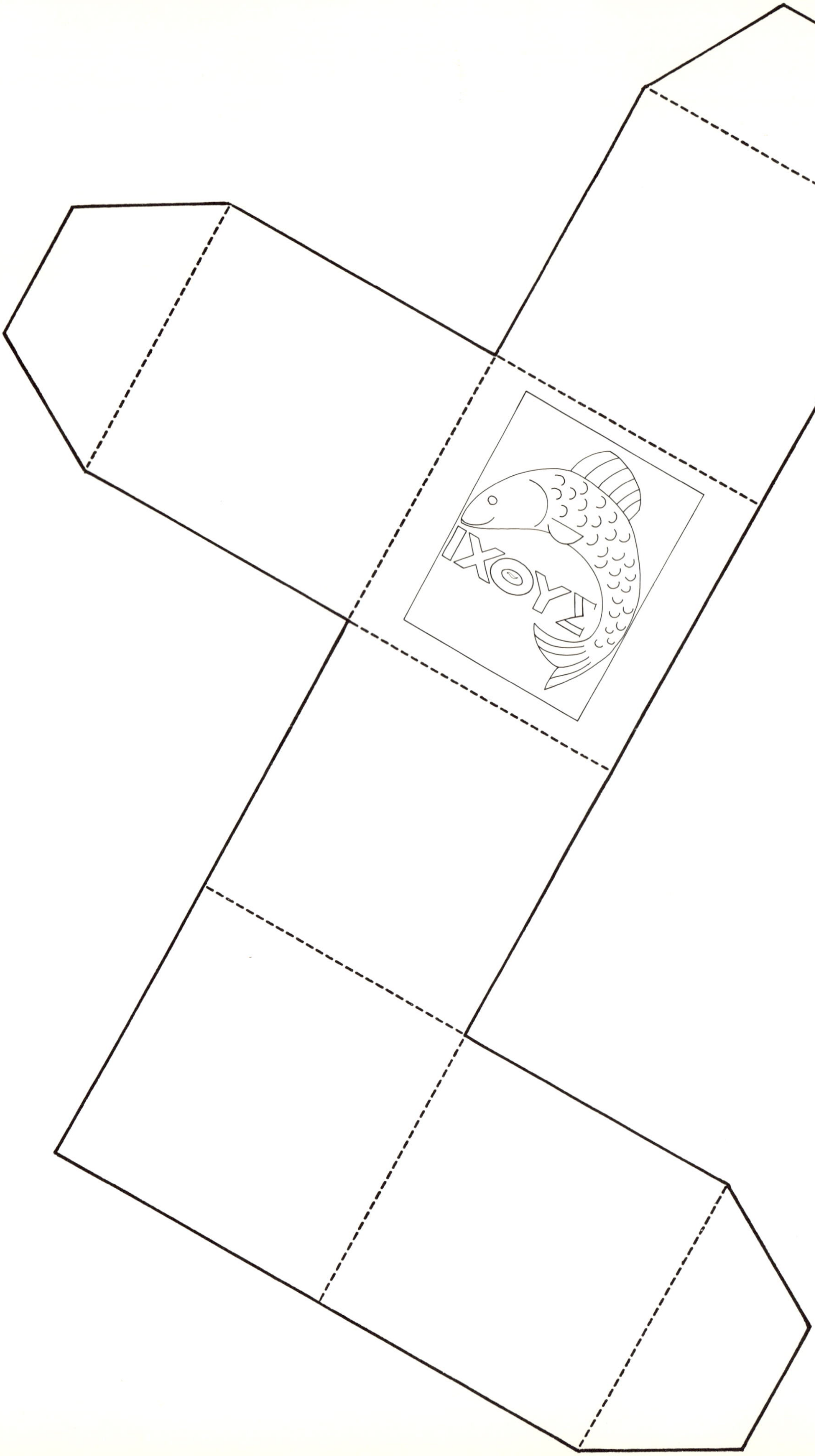
IXΘYΣ

God's Pledge of Ownership

. . . when you heard the true message, the Good News that brought you salvation, you believed in Christ, and God put his stamp of ownership on you by giving you the Holy Spirit he had promised. *Ephesians 1:13*

Janie and her mother walked down the aisle of the little church. Janie could hardly keep from skipping, she was so excited. She had never been to a wedding before, and she was especially glad when the usher showed them to a pew near the front. Janie could see everything.

After the wedding and reception, when Janie was riding home in the car with her mother, she leaned back on the seat and gave a long sigh. "You know, Mommy," she said, "it was so beautiful. Do you know what part I liked the very best of all?"

"Eating the wedding cake at the reception?" asked her mother with a smile.

"Maybe that was next-best," said Janie, "but the very best was when Tom put the ring on Mary's finger and said, 'With this ring I thee wed.' It was like he was giving her his heart forever."

The wedding ring is a beautiful symbol of the love and devotion between two people. When we believe in Jesus, God gives us something special. This something special is not an object like a ring, but it is his Holy Spirit. God's own Spirit comes to stay with us. This Holy Spirit helps us to be loving and kind to others. Then they know that we belong to God, that he loves us and we love him. Let's thank God today for the wonderful gift of his Holy Spirit.

A Faith That Stands

I ask God, from the wealth of his glory, to give you power through his Spirit to be strong in your inner selves. *Ephesians 3:16*

Two great oak trees stood on a grassy hill just outside of town. Everyone called them Twin Oaks, and men from the Forest and Parks Service said the trees were at least 250 years old. Tourists came to the little town just to see the Twin Oaks. Everyone loved the trees and wondered if they'd live another 250 years.

But one morning as the townspeople got up and went about their chores, they discovered that one of the giant trees had crashed to the ground. A great crowd gathered. A Parks Service man arrived. He studied the tree which had split apart and now lay on the ground. He shook his head and spoke to the people.

"We were afraid this might happen. This tree was struck by lightning several years ago. It's been slowly rotting away inside. You can see for yourselves—there was nothing left solid on the inside. We didn't know it was this bad, though." He turned to the other tree which still stood proudly. "Our tests show that the other tree is solid. It is very healthy and should last many more years."

People need to be strong inside, too—strong in their faith. In our Bible verse today, Paul was writing to some people who were beginning to feel unsure about Jesus. Paul prayed that these people, through God's power, would be strong in their inner selves, that is, in their faith. Then other people could not upset them and keep them from loving God and others. Let's pray that God will keep our faith strong so that we can stand up to troubles and temptations. Then, like the solid tree, we will be a joy for others.

How to Love Others

Be humble, gentle, and patient always. Show your love by being helpful to one another.
Ephesians 4:2

"George, it's been a week since your birthday. Don't you think it's time you wrote a thank-you note to Grandma for the ship model?"

"Aw, Mom," George protested, "I never know what to say. You can tell her I like it when you write to her."

Mother stepped in front of the TV set. "One short note. It'll mean so much to Grandma. Her days are pretty lonely and mail is a big help. Don't you love her?"

"Sure I love her," said George, getting up from in front of the TV. "But writing letters is hard."

Mother handed him a piece of paper and a pencil. George sat down at the dining room table to write.

It's so much easier to say we love someone than to do something that shows that love. But today's Scripture says that we should show love "by being helpful to one another." This is what George's mother asked of him; a thank-you note would be a helpful thing in Grandma's life. Would George take time to write that note? Will we take the time and trouble to help each other in our families? There's a clue in the first part of our Scripture. That part says, "Be humble, gentle, and patient always." This is the kind of person we need to be if we are going to be able to show love. Then we won't always be rushing ahead, thinking only of what we want. If we are patient and gentle with those in our families, we will be able to see ways of helping them.

With All That Power We Can Still Go Wrong

. . . do not make God's Holy Spirit sad. . . . Get rid of all bitterness. . . . No more shouting or insults. No more hateful feelings of any sort. *Ephesians 4:30-31*

Dad switched on the TV set and settled down with Steve to watch the Superbowl football game.

"Boy, oh boy, those Colts better win," he said, rubbing his hands together. Then he frowned. "Say, where's the picture? The set ought to be warmed up by now."

Steve made sure the set was plugged in, while Dad fiddled with the knobs. But the screen was blank, and there was no sound, either. "Let's see if we can watch with the Gibsons next door," Dad said.

At the neighbor's, Dad and Steve got to see the Colts win the Superbowl. And when Dad took the TV to be repaired, he was very relieved to find out that nothing major was wrong. A loose connection inside the set had kept the electricity from getting to where it was needed.

In this story something very minor kept the TV set from receiving the power it needed to work. We have said that God gives us a kind of power, too—the power of the Holy Spirit to share his love with others. But there are things that keep this power from working. Sometimes we make God's Holy Spirit sad because of what we do. Certainly something like committing a crime would make him sad, but even what we call little things can sadden the Holy Spirit and keep us from receiving the power for loving others. Shouting at each other, insulting someone, and having feelings of bitterness and hate can grieve God's Holy Spirit. But God, who knows us so well, knows that we all do these things. When he sent his Son, Jesus, to die for our sins, it was even for sins like these. The next time you shout at someone or have mean feelings, ask Jesus to forgive and help you. He can restore the power that turns hate to love and kindness.

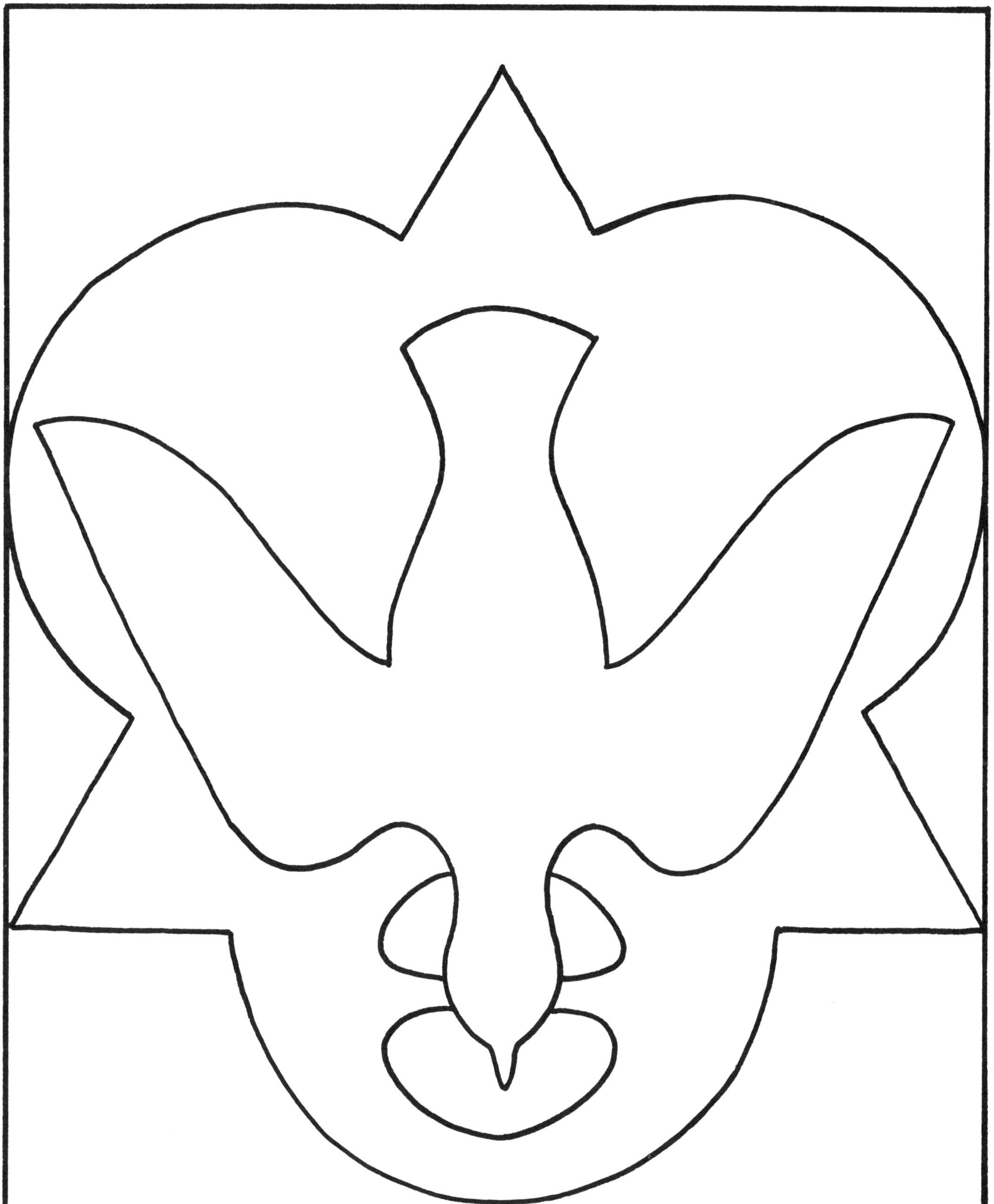

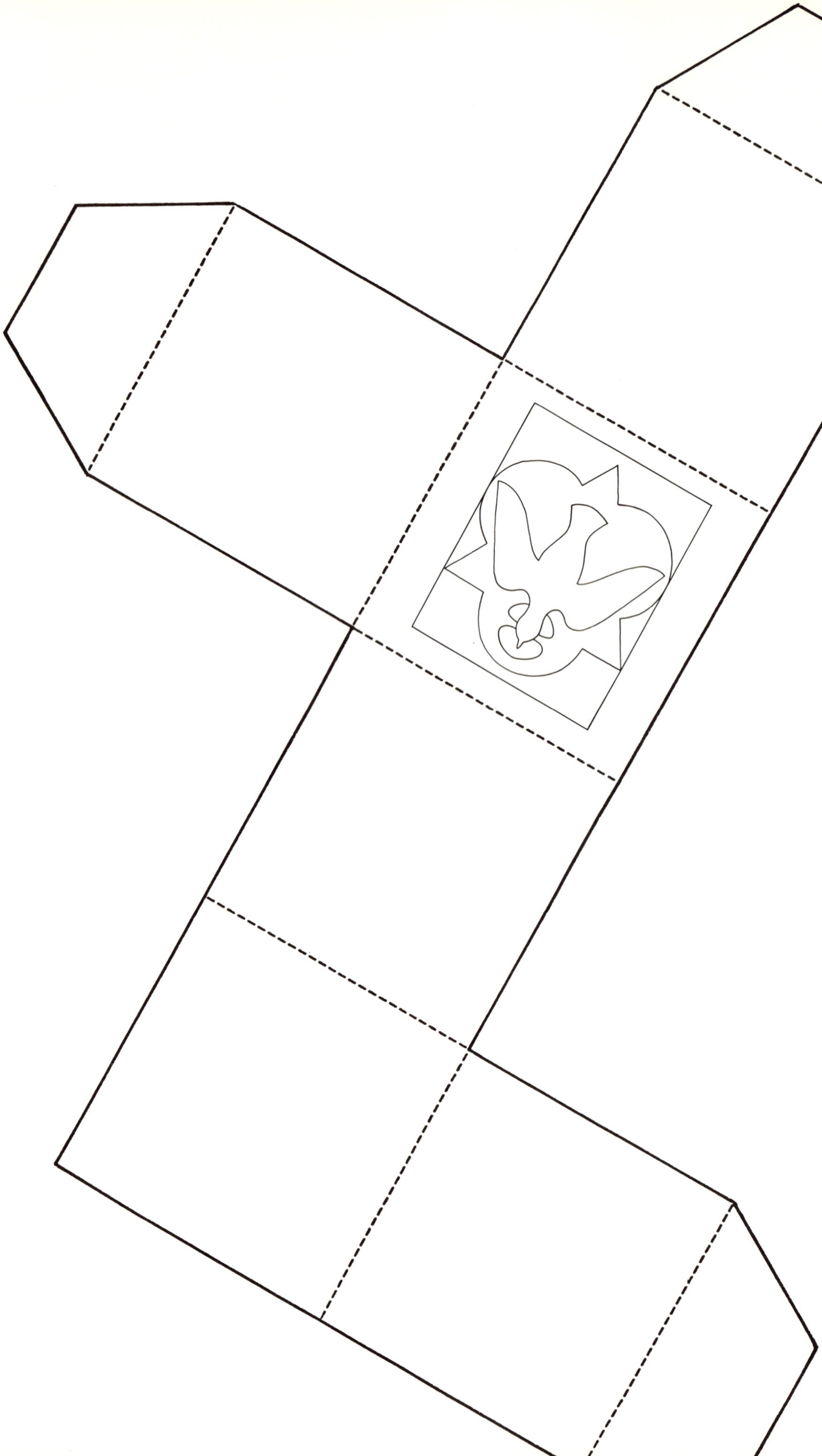

You're Important in God's Plan

In union with him [Christ] you too are being built together with all the others into a house where God lives through his Spirit. *Ephesians 2:22*

Tricia was helping her mom make cookies. She sat on a kitchen stool, reading the recipe while Mom mixed the ingredients.

"Cream one cup shortening," she read. "Add ¾ cup granulated sugar and ¾ cup brown sugar. Mix well." Tricia watched the mixer bowl go round and round while her mom scraped the sides. Then she read some more, "Add two eggs, one teaspoon of vanilla, and one-half teaspoon water." She stopped reading. "Half a teaspoon of water?" she repeated. "What's a little dab of plain old water going to do for our cookies?"

Mom laughed. "I really don't know," she said, "but recipes are tested many times before they're printed. You can be sure that even that little bit of water is important."

A half hour later, when the first batch of cookies was cool enough to eat, Tricia and her mom had a sample. The cookies were delicious. *Funny about that water,* Tricia thought. *It must do something.*

Even the smallest amount of something very ordinary can make a big difference, whether you're mixing cookie dough or constructing a huge building. Sometimes we feel small and ordinary when we think of all the people in the world. Or sometimes when we read about missionaries and evangelists and the work they are doing, we don't feel important at all. But our Scripture today talks about all Christians being part of a great building. Each Christian is an important part. The words say, "You, too." Even if you feel small, you can be happy knowing that you are an important part of God's plan.

Receiving God's Power

To him who is able to do so much more than we can ever ask for, or even think of, by means of the power working in us: to God be the glory . . . forever and ever! Amen.
Ephesians 3:20-21

It was two days before Christmas, and Pete and Carol were helping Dad with the Christmas tree. They climbed up and got the boxes of decorations out of the closet.

"I'll test the lights," said Pete.

Carol made sure there were hangers for each ornament.

"There," said Dad. "The tree's all set in the stand. Are you ready with those lights, Pete?"

Pete shook his head. "A blue one, a yellow, and a green are all out," he said.

"Did you make sure they were screwed in firmly?" asked Dad.

"Oh, didn't think of that." Pete tightened each light bulb. This time when he plugged in the set, every light lit up. In the evening the family sat around the tree, enjoying its beauty and the soft glow of its lights.

We know a light has to be plugged in in order to work. The bulb must be screwed into the socket firmly to receive the electric power that makes it give off light. Sometimes people talk about Christians being "plugged in" to God like a light is plugged into a socket. It's a good comparison. The Christian stays "plugged in" by staying close to God. He reads God's Word in the Bible and prays and worships with other Christians. He is then receiving power to love others and be a light for God. Even if you are a small child, you are receiving power that makes you special for others. Just think of how small a Christmas tree light is, but when the power is on, even that little light gives a glow that makes many others happy.

You Have a Specialty

Each one of us has been given a special gift. . . . *Ephesians 4:7*

Once there was a wise but very poor old man. He lived with his wife who was also very old and his little granddaughter who was only five. One year, in December, the old man knew he didn't have enough money to buy a Christmas present for his wife or granddaughter. He was so old it was hard for him to find work, but at last he found a part-time job sweeping the floors in the dime store. When he received his paycheck, he saved most of it for food. But he was able to buy Christmas gifts, too.

On Christmas morning his wife opened her package and discovered some red yarn and a pair of knitting needles. The granddaughter's package contained a coloring book and a box of crayons. The wife and granddaughter were delighted and set to work immediately. Before the day was over, the wife had knitted a pair of mittens for the little girl, and the little girl had surprised her grandmother with several very neatly colored pictures, which were hung on the wall.

The wise old grandfather just smiled and was happy. He knew that with the gifts he had given, the old woman and the little girl could then give something to each other.

Did you know that God gives us gifts that we can use for others, too? Our Bible verse says, "Each one of us has been given a special gift." Later in that chapter we read that these gifts are to be used in Christian service, that is, to help others know more of God's love. You have a special gift, a special ability, that you can use to help others. Perhaps you are very cheerful, can write thoughtful letters, or have a pleasant singing voice. You may work well with your hands or be good in sports. As you ask God to help you love others, he will show you ways to use your special gift.

We Fit Together like a Puzzle

Under his control all the different parts of the body fit together . . . when each separate part works as it should, the whole body grows and builds itself up through love.
Ephesians 4:16

"Randy, what are you going to do with those scissors?" asked his mother.

"Nothing," said four-year-old Randy as he headed for the family room.

Mother followed and watched from the doorway. Randy sat down at his little table. He grabbed a piece of a puzzle that was partly finished on the table. Before his mother could say, "Stop!" Randy had snipped off part of the puzzle piece.

"There," he said with satisfaction. "Now it fits."

"Randy, that's not the way to do a puzzle." Mother picked up the scissors from the table. "You can't force a piece to go where it doesn't belong."

But Randy was busy putting in puzzle pieces—they seemed to fit now. Then he came to the last piece. He twisted it every which way. There was nothing he could cut off to make it fit. The piece wasn't big enough; there was going to be a little hole left in the puzzle. Randy put his head down and cried.

This little boy had to learn the hard way that every piece in a puzzle has its proper place and its own work to do to make the whole picture. We could say that people are like parts of a puzzle, too. Each one is special in his or her own way. Just as God makes every snowflake different, he makes each of his people different. Each is important. We don't have to try to be like someone else. God needs us to be ourselves.

1976

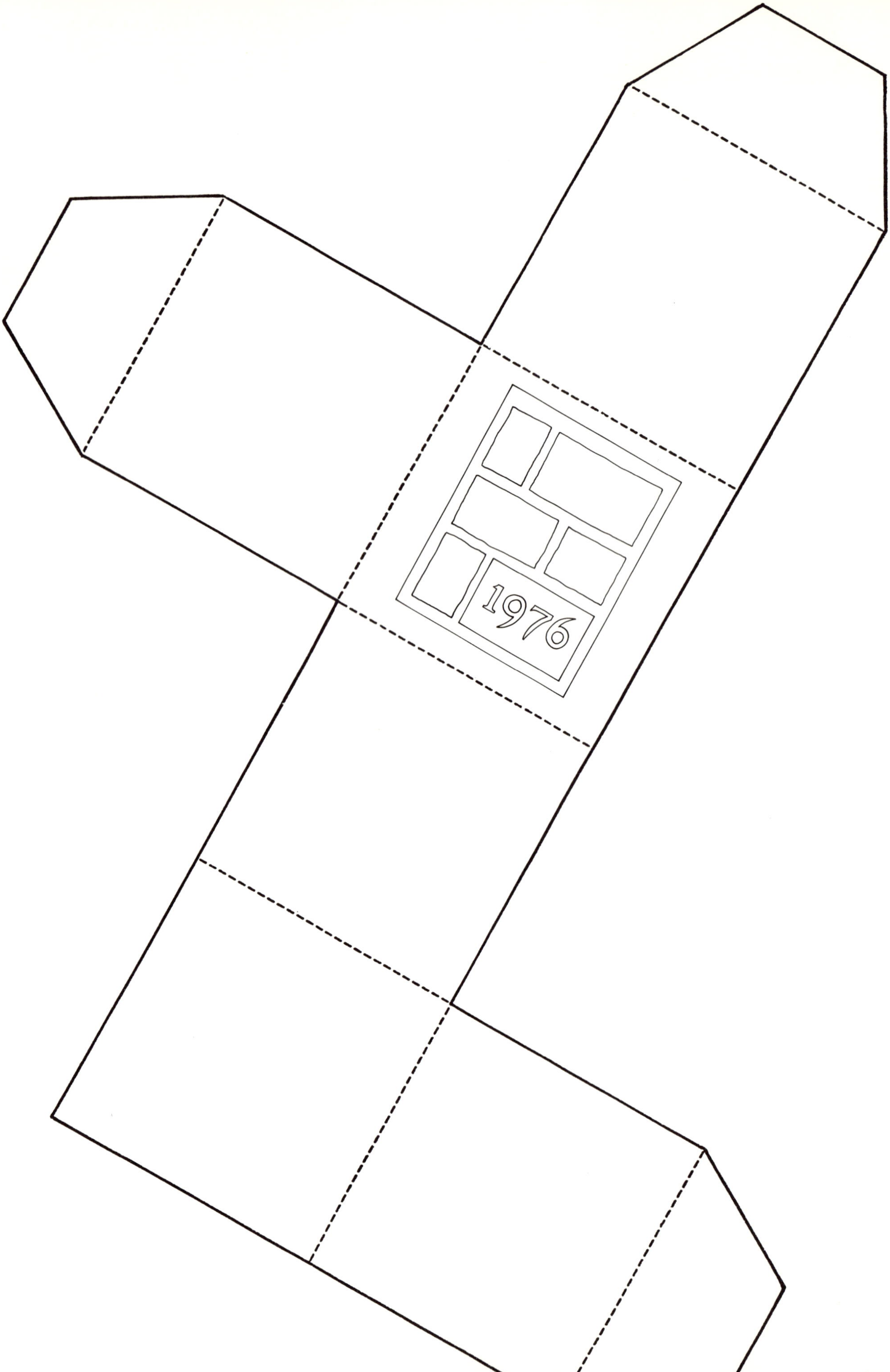
1976

Baptists, Lutherans, Methodists—Christians All

There is one Lord, one faith, one baptism; there is one God and Father of all men, who is Lord of all, works through all, and is in all. *Ephesians 4:5-6*

Sam walked over to the home of a new boy, Bill Grover, whom he'd met at school. He knocked on the door. "Want to come out and play catch?" he asked when Bill answered the door.

"Sure," said Bill. Pretty soon another boy came down the block. "Hey, it's my brother. Can he play, too?" Bill asked.

Sam was surprised. "Your brother? But he . . . he . . ."

"He looks Chinese?" Bill finished. "He was born in China, but he's my adopted brother." Bill grinned and pointed to a black girl just coming out of his house. "And that's Trina, my sister," he said.

Sam scratched his head. "You sure have a mixed-up family," he said.

Bill explained some more, "Our parents didn't have any children, so they thought they'd adopt some. We're all adopted. We look different, but we're all Grovers, just the same."

The Grovers had a lot of different sorts of people in their family. But all the children called Mr. Grover "Dad." There's a bigger family that has a lot of different sorts of people in it, too. It's the Christian family. All people everywhere who believe that Jesus is the Son of God and their Savior are Christians. We may have some differences. We may be Baptists, or Lutherans, or Methodists, or Presbyterians, or Catholics, or of another denomination. But the Scripture today reminds us that we are to look not for our differences, but for the ways we are the same. All Christians believe in the same God, and our faith is in his Son, Jesus. We share the family name of Christian, which is our most important name of all.

What to Do with Anger

If you become angry, do not let your anger lead you into sin; and do not stay angry all day. *Ephesians 4:26*

Eight-year-old Bill was working on a plastic airplane model that his sister had given him for his birthday. But try as he might, he couldn't get one wing to stay in place while the glue dried. He tried to hold it for a while. Then he tried to prop it in place. But the wing kept falling off. He became angrier and angrier. Finally, he took the plane and stuffed it into its box.

Storming into his sister's room, Bill threw the box down at her feet. "You can just keep that dumb old airplane. It's no good, anyway," he shouted. Tears ran down his face as he stomped out.

Tears came to his sister's eyes, too, as she picked up the broken model that had been smashed in anger.

We all become angry sometime or another. But we need to learn what to do about our angry feelings. Our Scripture tells us not to let anger lead us into sin. It's easy to see that's what happened to Bill—his anger led him to break his birthday present and be unkind to his sister. It's too bad he didn't think before he burst into anger and say, "I'm tired. I'll put this away and work on it later." Or he might have realized he needed help on that part of the model.

Some people say it's a good idea to count to ten before saying anything when we're angry. We can use this countdown as time to think about why we're angry and what we can do about it besides yelling. We can also pray when we're angry. Jesus has told us to come to him with all our problems. When we are angry, we certainly have a problem. Jesus will understand and he will help. He will help us to do something worthwhile about our anger so that we won't stay angry all day.

Feeling Ashamed Can Be a Good Thing

They have lost all feeling of shame; they give themselves over to vice, and do all sorts of indecent things without restraint. *Ephesians 4:19*

"Aren't you going awfully fast?" Hank cautioned his brother Bill who was at the wheel of the red sports coupé.

"Naw, it just seems like it 'cause you're not used to riding in class. You're used to that old junk heap of yours. Relax and enjoy a good ride," teased Bill.

"Well, I'd think you'd get your speedometer fixed so you'd be able to watch your speed. Hey! Look out! That car in front is stopping!"

Bill slammed on the brakes; there was a terrible screech and then CRASH!

Hank and his brother will be in the hospital a long time. So will the man who was in the car ahead.

Good drivers know that the speedometer should always be in working order. If a driver is going too fast and breaking the law, the speedometer warns him to slow down, obey the law, and be safe. People have a warning system, too. It's our conscience. When we do something wrong, our consciences make us feel ashamed. When we feel ashamed, we can come to God who forgives us for Jesus' sake and once more gives us the power to live his way. Our consciences are good to have. They bring us back to God so that we may live happily with him and others.

Our Scripture today speaks of people who don't care about God and don't believe his laws. They have been sinning so much that they don't even feel ashamed anymore. Like the car with the broken speedometer, these people with broken consciences break God's laws without knowing or caring. They are headed for real trouble. Let's thank God for the gift of a conscience and ask him to use it to help us live as his happy children.

What Words Can Do

Do not use harmful words in talking. Use only helpful words, the kind that build up and provide what is needed, so that what you say will do good to those who hear you.
Ephesians 4:29

"Shrimpy, shrimpy, you're a little shrimpy!" sing-songed Roger to Danny after school one day.

"'Sticks and stones will break my bones, but words will never hurt me!'" retorted Danny. He climbed on his bike and headed for home. When he got home, he flung his backpack of books on the floor. "That Roger makes me *so* mad," he grumbled.

Even though Danny had told Roger that words couldn't hurt him, Danny knew the words did hurt, maybe even *more* than sticks and stones. "Shrimpy, shrimpy"—how Danny hated it when the kids made fun of his being short. All afternoon those words echoed in his mind.

Sometimes we need to stop and think about what words can do. Words made Danny feel miserable. Words can also make us feel happy. Even words printed on a page can make us laugh or cry. The apostle Paul knew how important words can be. He tells us to use helpful words, words that will do good to those who hear them. The words of the Bible are very special since they tell us of God's love for us. These words make us strong as Christians, just as the food we eat builds our bodies. The most wonderful words ever spoken are the words of Jesus: "Your sins are forgiven." Jesus' words tell us that we are free from sin and death, that we can live happily as God's dear children. As we read God's Word we will be more able to use helpful words for our family and friends. Let's ask God to show us a time today when we can use words that will do good for someone else.

Forgiveness in Families

. . . be kind and tender-hearted to one another, and forgive one another, as God has forgiven you in Christ. *Ephesians 4:32*

"I'm not helping Sally with her math *anymore!*" said Linda, entering the kitchen. "She doesn't listen to a thing I say."

Dad looked up from the salad he was making. "That bad, huh?"

"Yes! She was crying and upset because she didn't understand reducing fractions. So I stopped working on *my* homework and very nicely went to help her. We did one problem; then she got all mad and said I didn't do it like the teacher. She can just flunk her old math!" Linda bit into a piece of raw carrot.

"Why don't you give her another chance?" asked Dad.

"Not unless she says she's sorry and that she'll really try."

Dad pointed with the carrot peeler to several slips of paper stuck on the refrigerator door. "See that top Bible verse?" he said.

Linda walked over to the refrigerator and read aloud, "'Be kind and tender-hearted to one another, and forgive one another, as God has forgiven you in Christ.'"

Dad nodded. "You know, one of the hardest things to do is to say you're sorry when you think you're in the right. But sometimes Christians need to do that. It's part of being kind and tender-hearted."

"But what have I got to be sorry for? Sally's the one who got all mad and told me I wasn't doing it right," Linda protested.

"Maybe you could forgive her for that, even though she hasn't said she's sorry. Maybe you could say you're sorry you got mad and stomped off."

Linda looked back at the Bible verse. *God's always forgiving me,* she thought. *Even now, I guess.* She walked slowly to Sally's room and knocked on the door. "Sally, I'm sorry I got mad and left. Want to try the math again?"

Sally opened the door, wiping her red eyes with the back of her hand. The other hand held a crumpled up math paper. "I'm sorry, too," she whimpered. "Thanks for coming back."

An Example to Follow

Since you are God's dear children, you must try to be like him. *Ephesians 5:1*

Little Timmy walked along the beach with his father. When his dad stooped to pick up an interesting shell, so did Timmy. When Dad put his hands in his pockets, Timmy stuffed his pudgy hands into the pockets of his corduroy jeans. Timmy looked at his dad's footprints in the damp sand. He stretched out his legs trying to take big steps, too. Timmy thought his dad was wonderful. He wanted to be like his dad and do the things his dad did.

You've probably seen little children like Timmy copying what an older person was doing. Sometimes we all try to do things the way someone else does. We may want to wear our hair in the style of a TV performer we admire, or when playing baseball we may copy the pitching style of our favorite pitcher. We may not realize we are copying someone. We admire that person so much that unconsciously we try to be like him or her.

This is what our Scripture is talking about today. "Since you are God's dear children, you must try to be like him." How can we be gentle and humble and loving as God's Son, Jesus, was? By getting to know him better and better. As we learn about him in the Bible, we get to know him better. We love him because he loved us and died for us so that we could be God's forgiven children. Just as little Timmy watched his dad and tried to copy his father's ways, so as we study about Jesus, we will find that we will want to be like Jesus and copy his ways. The wonderful part is that God will help us. If we pray for help in loving others and being gentle like Jesus, we will find God's power is helping us.

What Is Love?

Your life must be controlled by love, just as Christ loved us and gave his life for us. . . .
Ephesians 5:2

"I don't know why Aunt Bessie had to pick tonight to come over," Janet grumbled to her mother. "It always happens on my favorite TV night."

"Now, Janet, you know Aunt Bessie needs company now and then," Mother said.

Janet nodded and went up to her room, grumbling under her breath. Aunt Bessie could talk louder and longer than anyone else in the world. Whenever she came over, no one could watch TV; the whole family had to sit around listening to Aunt Bessie. *So what if Aunt Bessie lives alone and doesn't have any other family since Uncle Tom died. You'd think she could pick a different night to visit,* Janet thought.

It's so easy to be like Janet. We all have little pleasures we enjoy, and we get put out if we have to miss one because of another person's need. But God wants us to take our eyes off ourselves and what we want and look out at other people. Perhaps Aunt Bessie's need for talk and company was much greater than Janet's need for TV. To let our lives be controlled by love, as the Scripture says today, we need to be looking at the needs of those around us. This is what Christ did when he was here. He saw people alone and without God. He wanted them to know God's love, to be forgiven and able to live as God's children. He went about helping and healing and sharing God's love. His life and death were for others. What a far-reaching love this is! Today, if we think about this love, we can take our eyes off ourselves and see the needs of the people around us.

Why Bother to Work Hard?

Do your work . . . cheerfully, then, as though you served the Lord, and not merely men.
Ephesians 6:7

If there was one thing Betsy disliked, it was making her bed and tidying up her room in the morning. She usually tossed her pajamas on the floor of the closet along with anything else in sight and pulled up her bedspread, pushing it around the lumps in the covers. One morning she awoke because of a strange smell coming from the kitchen. It wasn't a breakfast smell; it was—popcorn! Hurray! Mother must have run out of potato chips for the lunch sacks, so she was making popcorn instead. Then, as Betsy was dressing, she smelled bacon and French toast. What a good morning! Betsy was so pleased that she hung her pajamas on their hook, smoothed out the bed wrinkles before pulling up the spread, and even put her dirty clothes in the hamper. Full of good cheer, she bounded downstairs to breakfast.

Isn't it true that when someone does something that pleases you, you want to do something pleasing in return? Betsy was happy about all the good things her mother was cooking—so happy that she cheerfully tidied up her room and did an especially good job. This will help us understand our Bible verse for today, which says we should do our work cheerfully, as if doing it for the Lord. The Lord does so much for us: he forgives us for Jesus' sake; he brings us his peace and answers our prayers; he is always our friend. Next time you have some work to do that you feel grumpy about, think about the Lord. He's done so much for you. Can't you do this task cheerfully—for him?

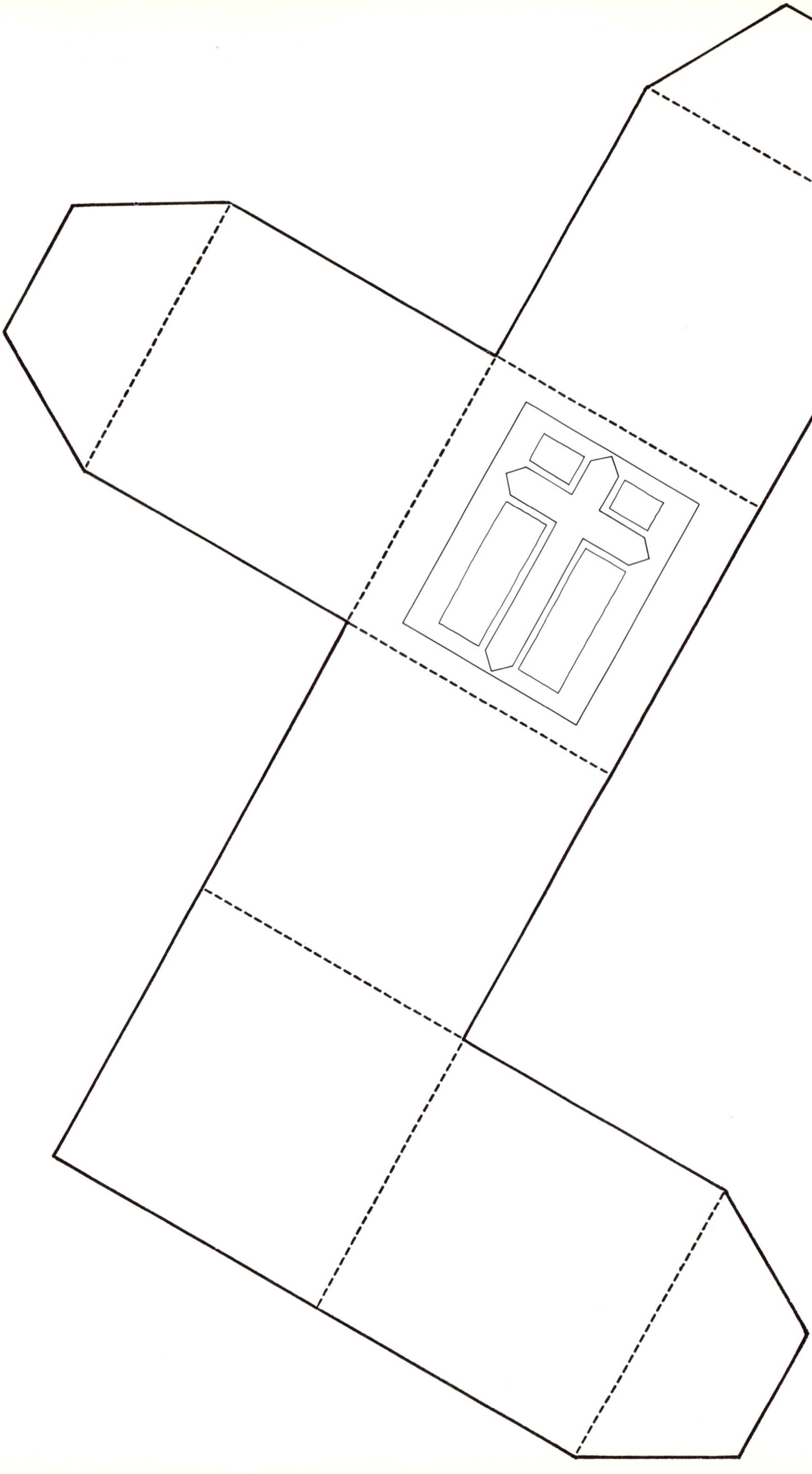

How to Know God's Will

Try to learn what pleases the Lord. *Ephesians 5:10*

"I'm never going to mow Old Man Wilson's lawn again," complained Bruce to his dad. "You just can't please that man."

"Oh?" said Dad, looking up from the hedge he was clipping.

"The first time I cut his grass, Mr. Wilson said that my lawn mower blade was too low. So the next time I raised the blade. Then he said I hardly cut the grass at all, and he wasn't going to pay full price. Today he said I wasn't getting close enough to the flower beds, but last week he had a fit thinking I was going to run over his petunias."

Dad started clipping again. "Some people are just hard to please," he said.

Bruce put the lawn mower away. "Well, if Mr. Wilson would make up his mind about what he wants, it would help."

There are people young and old like Mr. Wilson—hard to please. These people don't seem to know what they want. But the Lord Jesus knows what he wants. (He loves us so much he died for our sins.) Naturally, we want to see what we can do to please him. And he is clear about it in his Word. In the Old Testament Book of Micah we read, "What does the Lord require of you but to do justice, and to love kindness, and to walk humbly with your God?" God has not changed his mind since those times. He is still pleased when we are just and kind and humble. In another devotion in this book we read a New Testament verse about being the sort of person who is kind to others, tender-hearted, and forgiving. Now that we know what pleases God, we can look for opportunities at home, at school, or at work to do something pleasing to him. What might it be today?

Strong in Faith

Finally, build up your strength in union with the Lord, and by means of his mighty power. *Ephesians 6:10*

"Oh, boy, it came!" said Don, seeing the package on his front steps.

"What came?" asked his friend Barney, as the boys set their schoolbooks down on the steps.

Don ripped open the package. "My Super-New Muscle Builder for superstrong muscles," said Don. "I ordered it out of my *Muscle Man Magazine.*"

"Really gonna get with it, huh?" said Barney, trying to hide a grin. He knew how much other muscle-building equipment gathered dust in Don's room.

"You wait. Two weeks of working out with this and I'll be a new man."

"I'll wait," said Barney.

Don certainly did a lot of talking about getting strong. But apparently that's all he ever did about it, and muscles won't get superstrong without work. Our faith doesn't get strong by itself, either. Paul says we build a strong faith "in union with the Lord, and by means of his mighty power." God's power is what builds our faith. His power works through his Word which we find in the Bible. God's Word is the strength builder for our faith. As we hear this Word in church and church school and talk about what God has done for us in our families, our faith becomes stronger. Don's muscles wouldn't become strong if he never used his muscle-building equipment. Let's not let our faith become weak. Let's use the faith-building equipment God has given us—his own wonderful Word.

Use Your Protection

Put on all the armor that God gives you, so that you will stand up against the Devil's evil tricks.
Ephesians 6:11

Mr. Williams was looking over the new cars in the automotive showroom. He kicked the tires of a yellow hardtop convertible, then peered inside.

"A beauty, isn't it, sir?" said a salesman, coming up to Mr. Williams. "All that safety equipment you see is included, you know. Costs nothing extra."

"Never use a seat belt or safety harness myself," grumbled Mr. Williams. "Doesn't have to be there as far as I'm concerned."

"Oh . . . well . . . ah, notice our new recessed instrument panel and body-form bucket seats," said the salesman.

Two weeks later a picture of Mr. Williams's new car was in the newspaper. The front end was bashed in. Underneath the picture the caption read, "The car's driver, Mr. J. Williams, suffered multiple injuries. He was not wearing a seat belt."

Mr. Williams didn't care if the safety equipment was free or not. He wasn't going to use it. It's too bad; the equipment might have saved him from serious injury. God gives us some safety equipment, too. The Scripture calls it "armor" to withstand the Devil's tricks. As we go about in our daily lives at school and home, we are often tempted to do or say wrong things. Using our armor will help keep us from evil. What is this armor? Truth, righteousness, faith, the readiness to tell others about God's wonderful love—these are the components of our armor. Each day we put on our armor by remembering the truth that God loves us and sent Jesus as our Savior. We put on the armor of righteousness by remembering that it is Jesus' righteousness that is ours. And, as we are ready to tell others of God's love, evil will not be able to push its way into our minds.

The Power of the Word of God

And accept salvation for a helmet, and the word of God as the sword that the Spirit gives you.
Ephesians 6:17

Billy and Betty were little twins watching a football game on TV with their dad. They didn't know much about the game and complained that they couldn't tell who had the ball. Suddenly Dad cheered and sat forward in his chair.

"An interception!" exclaimed Dad. "Now *our* team has the ball!"

"How come all those fellows quit playing and that other bunch came in?" asked Billy.

"Maybe they got mad and quit," said Betty.

"No," laughed Dad. "The first bunch was the *defensive* team. They have to keep the other side from making a score. Now that our team has the ball, our *offensive* team goes in. They'll try to move the ball forward down the field to make a touchdown."

Let's remember this story while we talk about today's Scripture. Yesterday we talked about armor that protects us from evil. That armor is truth, righteousness, readiness, and faith; today we add our salvation, which is called a helmet. All of these are our *defensive* equipment that keeps evil from getting hold of us. But how are we to move forward in our lives to do the good that God wants us to do? We need *offensive* equipment. A sword is an offensive weapon, and this is what the apostle Paul calls the Word of God. God's powerful Word is our sword against evil. As we read the Bible and remember how Jesus died for our sins and now comes to us in love to stay with us each day, we have power to be the offensive team for God. We *can* love others and help them. And as we speak God's Word to others, that Word can help them to know God, too.

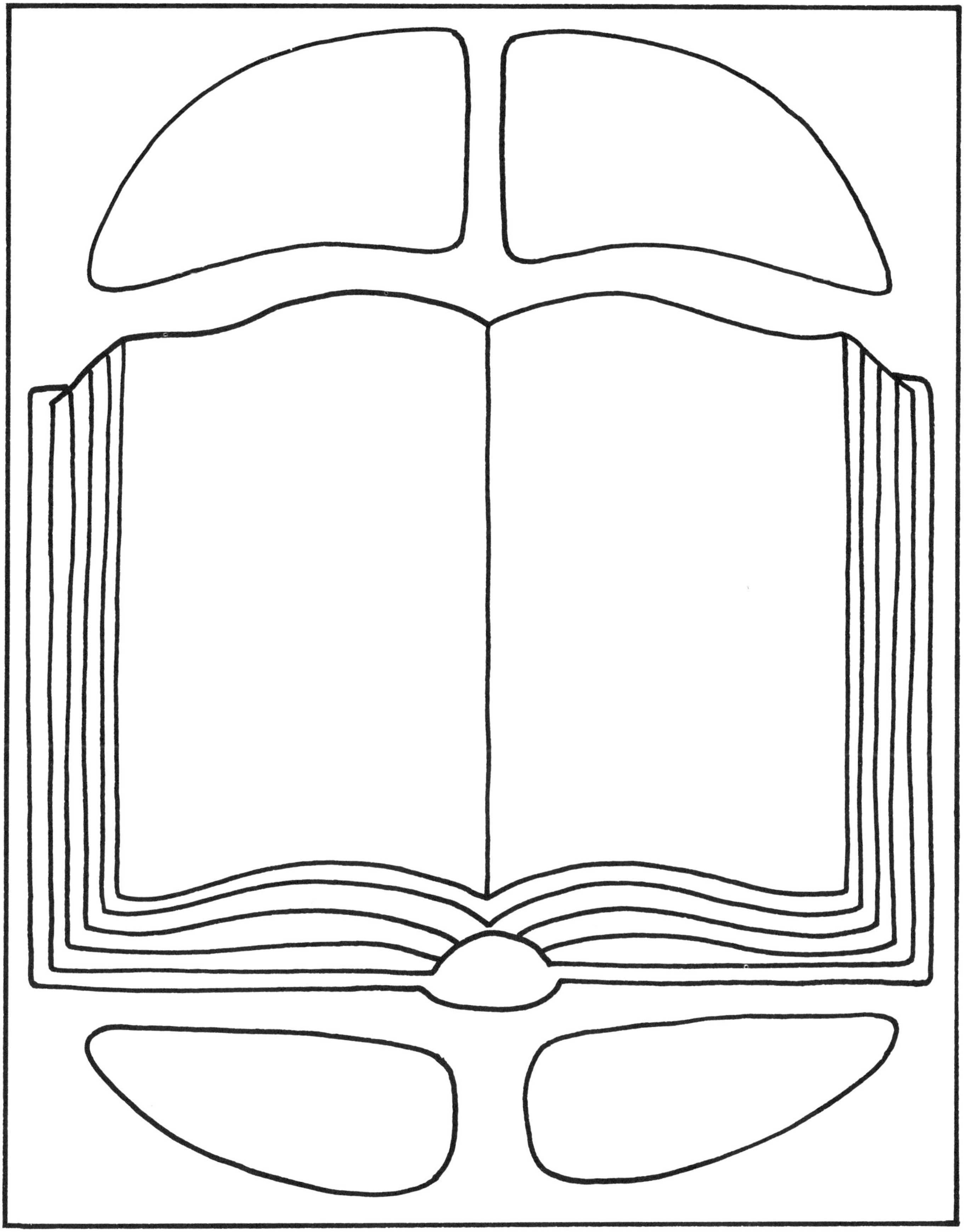

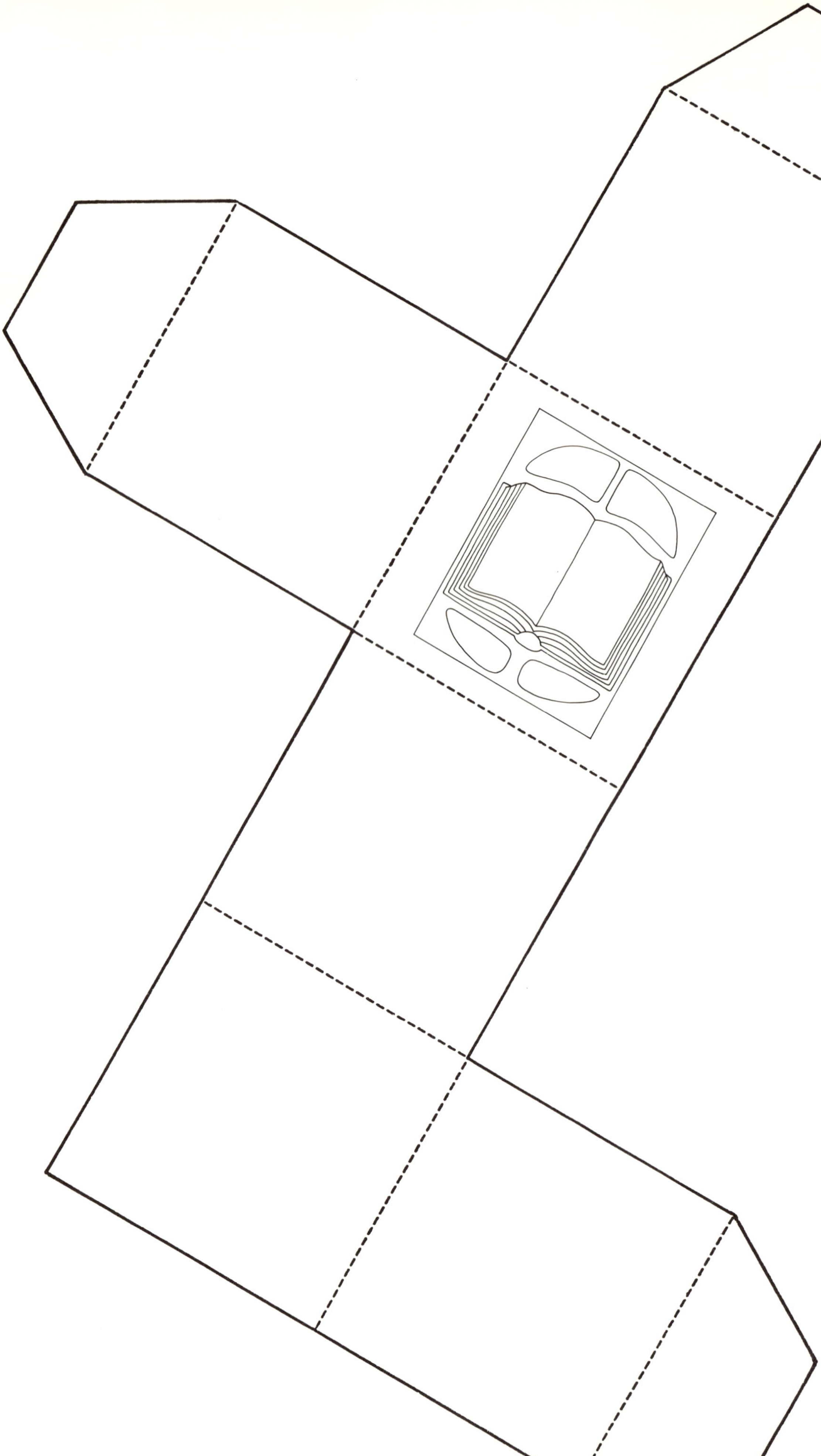

Being Thankful When It's Hard

Always give thanks for everything to God the Father, in the name of our Lord Jesus Christ. *Ephesians 5:20*

On the day before Thanksgiving a newspaper reporter went out into the streets to ask people what they were thankful for. "Well, I don't know," said one, "prices are so high, but at least turkey is cheap. That's something, I guess." A young sailor thought over the question and shook his head. "Not one single thing," he said and grumbled about life in the service. A newspaper on a nearby newsstand showed a picture of a starving child in a famine-swept country. Yet here on the street of a prosperous country stood a healthy, employed young man who said he had absolutely nothing for which to be thankful.

We shake our heads and think, *Shame on that young man!* Yet aren't there times when we all think only of the things we want and forget all we have? How grumpy children become when Mother cooks a dinner they don't like! How grumpy parents become when the weather is wet or cold! Somedays we find ourselves complaining about everything. At times like this, sit down and write a list of all the things you're unhappy about. Then make a list of all the things you can be glad about. You may be surprised how long the glad list will be. Why not try it today? Start the glad list with the fact that Jesus is your Savior, then list all the blessings he brings. When you finish your list, you will be able to thank God for everything, even unhappy things, as you see how these draw you closer to God and make the blessings even more special.

Keep the Hot Line Open

. . . Pray on every occasion, as the Spirit leads. . . . *Ephesians 6:18*

"You know, it's Grandma's birthday," Mom said to Doris. "Let's call her long distance and wish her happy birthday." Mom picked up the receiver to dial direct. "Oh, dear, a busy signal." In a few minutes she tried again.

A voice came on the line. "The number you have reached has been disconnected. Please check the number you are dialing."

"Maybe I dialed wrong," said Mom. She dialed once more, very carefully.

"The number 224-6178 has been changed to 224-6032. Please make a note of this new number," a voice said.

"Oh, dear," said Mom. "I guess Grandma forgot to send me her new number." After ten minutes of trying, Mom and Doris finally got Grandma on the line.

Has something like this ever happened to you? Maybe when you were only trying to call a friend in your neighborhood? Aren't you glad it's not that difficult to talk with our Lord? Talking with God in prayer is much easier than talking on a telephone, even when the phone works perfectly. There are times when we will want to kneel in a quiet place and talk with God for a long time. But there are other times during our busy days when we can pray short prayers, even one- or two-word prayers. The Bible says we should "pray on every occasion." In the middle of a baseball game or riding down the street on your bike can be times for prayer. Praying to God about everything in our lives and for all people around us helps us to remember that God cares about everything we are doing. He loves us and wants to share our lives. When reading in the Gospels, you'll notice how often Jesus prayed. And because we believe in him and pray in his name, we can know that God's line will never be busy to us; we will never get a wrong number when calling on our heavenly Father.

Pray for Your Pastor

And pray also for me, that God will give me a message, when I am ready to speak, that I may speak boldly and make known the gospel's secret. *Ephesians 6:19*

The Smiths were planning their Christmas list. They talked about what they would give to the neighbors and what charities they would support. They wanted to be sure to give to the needy. But when six-year-old Doug said, "I think I'll give Mrs. Starkweather some of my dried parsley," everyone laughed.

"Mrs. Starkweather? She's so rich she probably doesn't even know parsley when she sees it. You could give it to her cook," laughed Doug's sister.

But Doug filled a little bottle with some of the dried parsley from his garden and took it to Mrs. Starkweather's house. The butler said he'd put it under the Christmas tree.

After Christmas a small envelope came in the mail for Doug. He opened it and took out a folded note printed with the name Mrs. George R. Starkweather III. Doug's mother read the note out loud: "Dear Douglas, You cannot know how deeply I appreciate your gift of parsley. So often my Christmas mornings are lonely, but my heart was warmed when I realized a little boy down the street had thought of me. Please come Tuesday afternoon at three o'clock for Christmas cookies and milk. Sincerely, Mrs. Starkweather."

Although Mrs. Starkweather seemed to have everything, her need was as great as that of the poor people on the Smiths' Christmas list. Doug was thoughtful not to forget someone who seemed to have everything. We need to be like Doug with our prayers, too. Of course we pray for those who don't know the Lord, and for those in our families, and for others close to us; but sometimes we forget to pray for our pastors. These men are rich in faith; do they need our little prayers? Oh, yes! Read again the Scripture for today written by Paul, a great man of faith, who realized his own need for the prayers of others. We are all one family of Christians. Prayer helps keep our family united and strong.

How to Pray for Others

I ask that your minds may be opened to see his light, so that you will know what is the hope to which he has called you, how rich are the wonderful blessings he promises his people. *Ephesians 1:18*

Lisa was baby-sitting with four-year-old Andy. While Lisa was trying to get Andy to bed for the third time that evening, Andy asked for another drink of water.

"No," Lisa said firmly. "You've had two glasses already. That's enough."

Then thinking a minute, Andy plopped down on the floor beside his bed. "You didn't hear all my prayer. I have some more," he said.

Lisa sat on the bed with her hands folded and her eyes closed.

Andy prayed, "Please make Tommy give back my dump truck, and don't let Johnny get to nursery school first. He always gets the best crayons. Amen."

In his way, Andy was praying about the things that were really bothering him. Jesus told us to pray about all our troubles. But he also wants us to learn to pray in a special way for others. Paul, in the Bible verse for today, is telling some people how he is praying for them. We can learn a lot from Paul because he loved the Lord very much and worked hard to help others know Jesus. Paul says that in his prayers he asks that people come to know and understand God more and more. Paul knows that the more people know and love God, the happier they will be and the more they will love other people. Perhaps you have a problem with another person as Andy did. Why not pray that that person will know more of God's wonderful love? Then you will be praying like Paul.

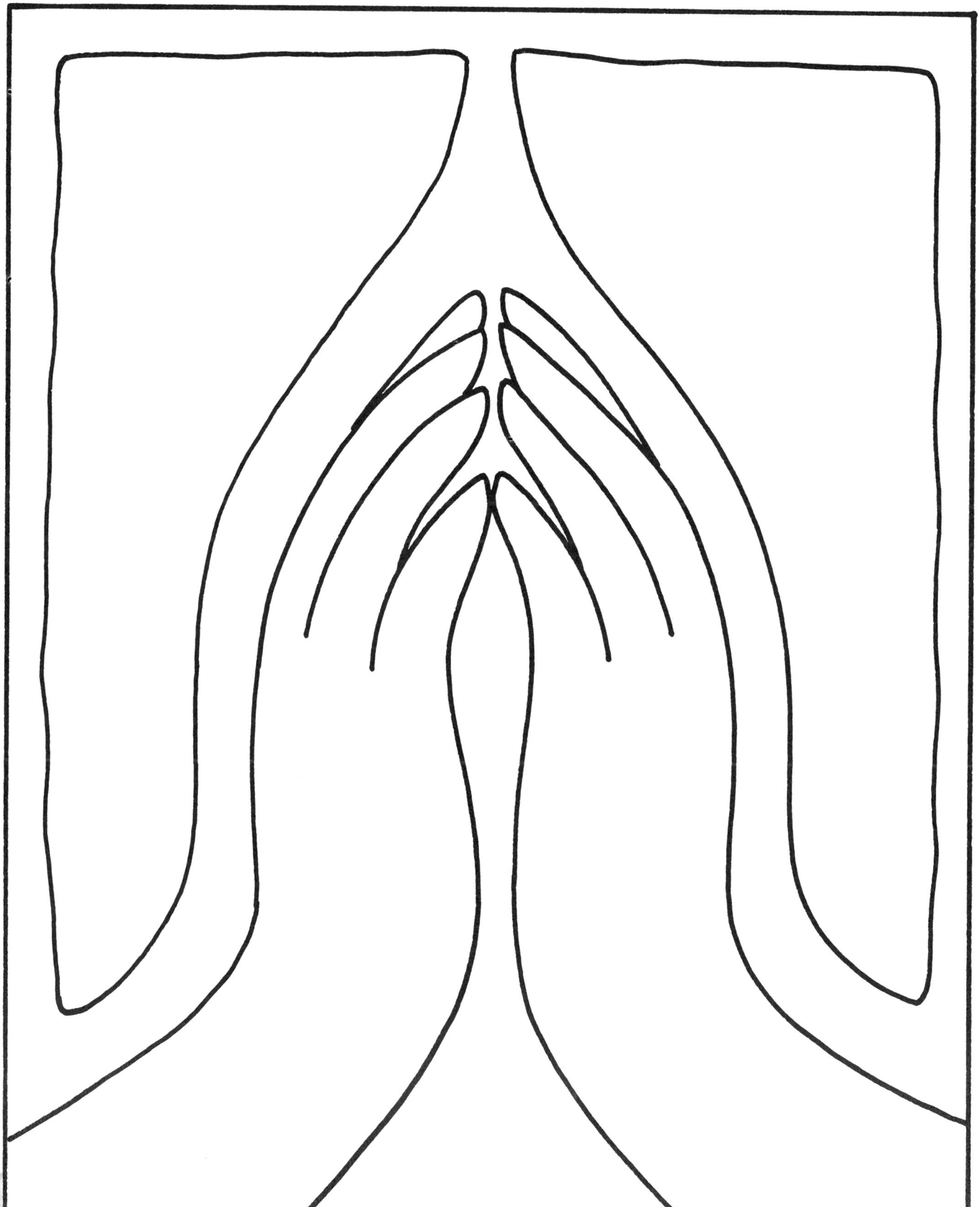

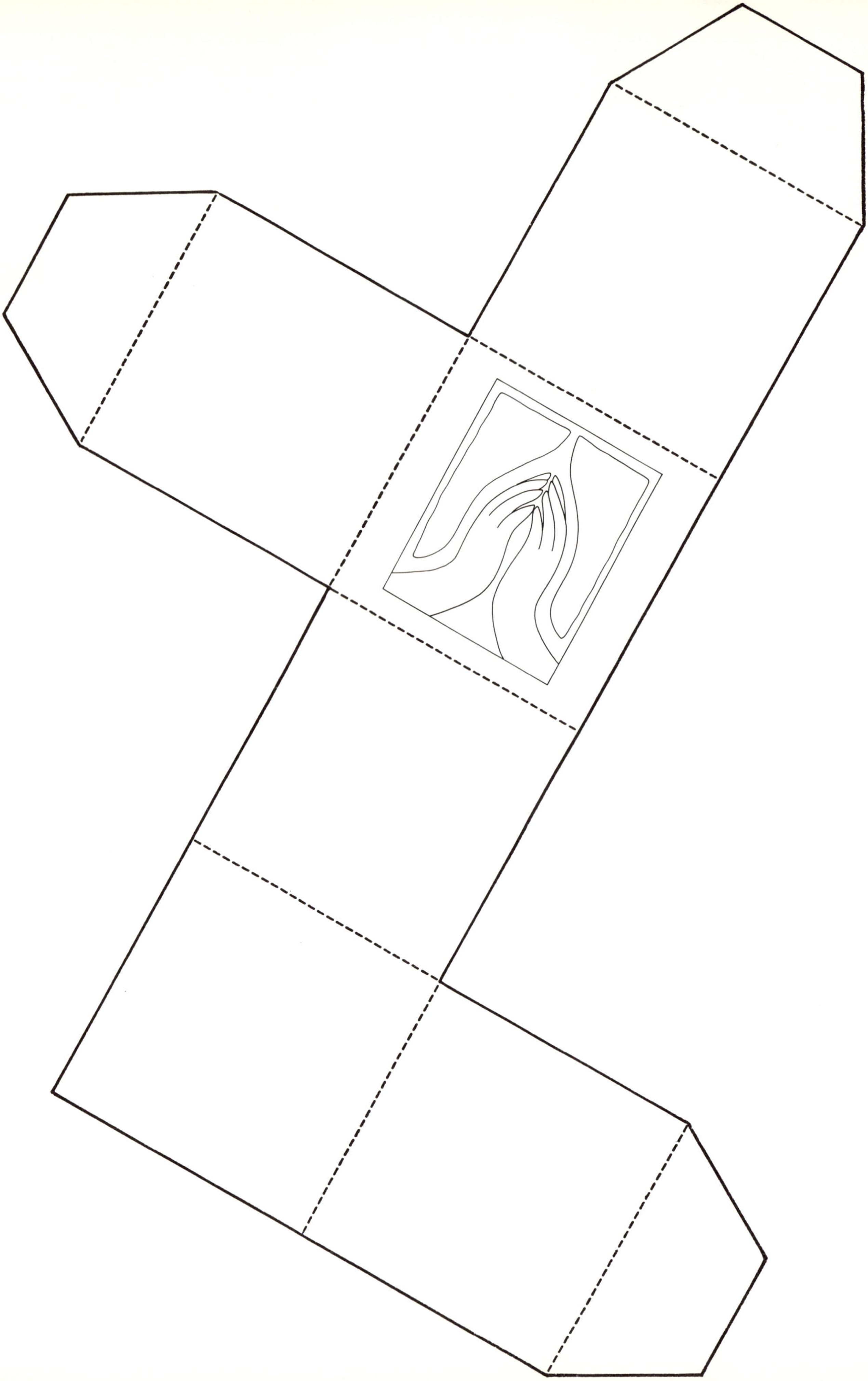

Giving In in Love

Submit yourselves to one another, because of your reverence for Christ.

Ephesians 5:21

Mary and Hilda were working on a poster for Sunday school. They had drawn a picture of baby Jesus in the manger and some cows nearby.

"My cow's going to be black," said Mary, reaching for a crayon.

"Mine's going to be brown and white like the ones I've seen in the fields," Hilda said. "The manger ought to be brown," she added.

"Oh, no. Gray," said Mary.

"Who ever heard of a gray manger?" asked Hilda.

"The old boards would be gray," Mary replied.

"The mangers I've seen in pictures are always brown," Hilda said firmly.

The girls' voices got louder and louder. Finally Hilda threw down her crayon. "You can just do the ol' poster yourself," she yelled.

How sad for both girls that neither one was willing to give in. But then, isn't that the way people are so often? Isn't that what causes arguments and fights—people wanting things their own way? Our Scripture says that Christians are to be different. "Submit yourselves to one another," the verse says. Other Bible translations say, "Fit in with one another" and "Give way to one another." Christians don't always have the same ideas about everything, but they do love Jesus. Because of our love for him, we are to give in to each other. As we remember how much Jesus loves us, how he lived and died and rose again that we could be forgiven and know God, we can let go of our own ideas and not have to have everything go our way. Because Jesus gave up his life for us, now we can give up our way for each other.

God's Plan for Wives

Wives, submit yourselves to your husbands, as to the Lord. *Ephesians 5:22*

In the last minute of the final quarter of the girls' basketball game, the score was tied: Rockville 62—Waterville 62. Sheila was a guard for Waterville. She waved her hands wildly in front of the girl from Rockville who had the ball. The Rockville girl couldn't shoot. She passed the ball across the court to a teammate. Suddenly Sheila ran across the court to guard the other girl, leaving her own area unguarded. The ball came back to this area. A Rockville forward shot. A basket! The final whistle blew, and Rockville won, 64-62. Sheila felt miserable. If she had followed her captain's plan and had stayed in position instead of running across the court, maybe she could have blocked the winning shot.

On any kind of team, the members go along with what the captain says. If they have a different idea, they can talk it over with the captain, but he or she has the final say. This makes the team a strong unit instead of just a bunch of people, each going his or her own way. A family is like a team, a very special team, in which the husband is to be the captain. God's Word to us today says that wives should submit or adapt to their husbands. This means they should go along with their husbands' decisions. Wives help the family team to work smoothly together. Perhaps today could be a special day to pray for women you know who are wives—your mother, mothers of your friends, aunts, teachers. These wives have many responsibilities in their important place on the team.

God's Plan for Husbands

Husbands, love your wives in the same way that Christ loved the church and gave his life for it.
Ephesians 5:25

The ship slowly made its way through the choppy seas of the North Atlantic Ocean. Suddenly a mighty crash jolted the ship to a halt. Passengers fell out of their chairs and beds. What had happened? Then the word came: the ship had collided with an iceberg. Everyone was to put on a life jacket and come to the deck where the lifeboats were being made ready. An SOS had been sent, and another ship was near enough to be there in an hour. The ship listed to the port side. Would it stay afloat until all passengers and crew could get off in the lifeboats? Passengers screamed and babies cried as harried crewmen prepared the boats. And all the time the captain went about giving encouragement and directions. Finally, the last of the lifeboats was in the water; this one carried the crew. But one man stayed with the ship—the captain. There was a possibility the ship would not sink. He would do everything he could to save his ship. The captain worked hard and bravely. By the time the rescue ship arrived, the captain felt confident that his ship could be towed in when the seas calmed.

A captain of a ship is asked to give everything for his ship. The crew does their part and follows the captain's orders, but in the end, it is the captain who gives his all for his ship. In a much bigger way, Jesus Christ gave his all for his people, the church. And today, we see that this is what God asks of husbands. We have learned that God asks wives to adapt to their husbands' ways of doing things. Now we understand that a husband gives his whole self for his wife. In God's plan for families there is tremendous giving. People who do not know Christ's love may not understand, but Christian families know the love and forgiveness of Christ. This love passes in different ways from wives to husbands and from husbands to wives. This love builds solid families.

God's Plan for Children

Children, it is your Christian duty to obey your parents, for this is the right thing to do.
Ephesians 6:1

Kate and Dick were excited. Their mother cat had kittens. They had never before seen any tiny baby animals. The kittens now had their eyes open and were beginning to wander about. Every day after school Kate and Dick would sit on stools in the kitchen, eating a snack and watching the kittens in the cozy box with their mother. Sometimes the kittens would manage to crawl over the side of the box and plop down on the kitchen floor.

"Look at that one! He's almost to the dining room," said Dick. Then the children laughed as the mother cat calmly got out of the box, came over and picked up her kitten by the scruff of the neck, and returned him to the box. But away he went again. This time mother cat was firmer and gave her son a swat before returning him to the box.

"Just like a real mother," said Kate. "She really lets those kittens know how to behave."

Of course, what Kate meant is that animal mothers can sometimes be much like our own mothers. Even animal parents instruct their young so that the little ones won't get hurt and will know how to behave as they grow up. People are God's special creation. How much more important it is for parents to teach their children and for children to obey their parents! Christian parents learn from God. Then they want to pass on what they learn and how to live to their children. God has given parents this big responsibility. This is why Paul tells us today that the right thing for children to do is to obey their parents.

Watching Our Language

Nor is it fitting for you to use obscene, foolish, or dirty words. Rather you should give thanks to God. *Ephesians 5:4*

Beth and Paul had gone with their parents on vacation. It was good to get away from the city and enjoy the sand and water and beauty of the wilderness. One evening, the children sat on the beach watching the sun set. The sun was a huge ball of red gold, turning the clouds pink. The waves shimmered with golden highlights as they lapped the shore.

"Just think," said Beth, "God made it all. I want to remember this sight forever."

"Yeah," said Paul, "but look close at the water. Somebody sure has messed it up."

Beth then saw the slime and tar that were also rolling in with the waves. "Yuk!" she said.

"Probably some ship pumped its bilges. It's against the law to do that in so close, but some of them do it anyway and mess up what God made," said Paul.

Many people these days are very aware and concerned about the problem of pollution of our environment. We need to be concerned about another sort of pollution, too—pollution of our language. Swearing and using dirty words are nothing new. Even back when our Scripture was written, there were people who used bad words. If we look at the second part of the Scripture verse, we can understand better why we shouldn't swear. It says, "Rather you should give thanks to God." A person who is thankful to God for our beautiful world, for God's care, and for our Savior Jesus will want everything he does and says to show thanks to God. He will want his actions and words to help others to know of God's love. Swear words and dirty talk will never help others to know this love.

God's Word and Foolish Words

Do not let anyone deceive you with foolish words. . . . *Ephesians 5:6*

"Why don't you come over Sunday morning and we'll go hiking?" Warren asked.

"How about Sunday afternoon?" suggested Bob. "I go to church in the morning."

"Aw, you can skip it, can't you? My dad says that you're closer to God out in the woods than in a church," said Warren.

"I know sometimes it might feel like that," said Bob, "'cause you're out there with the trees and things God made. But God made people, too. Jesus died for people. It's good to get together on Sunday to thank God and learn more about him."

"Bet you don't understand half what goes on," scoffed Warren. "So why bother?"

"It's like a big family getting together. Even if I don't understand everything, it's a good feeling being with all God's family."

"Well, afternoon'll be okay for the hike, I guess," said Warren.

There are a lot of people around speaking foolish words about God as Warren was doing. Bob was wise not to let Warren change his thinking. This is what the Scripture means when it says, "Do not let anyone deceive you with foolish words." Warren said church didn't matter; other people will tell you it doesn't matter if you swear, take something from a store, or talk back to your parents. People who speak these foolish words do not know God and his Word. We know that doing wrong does matter; it matters so much that it keeps us away from God. But Jesus came that we could be forgiven and live close to God. If we continue to read and learn God's Word, people who speak foolish words about him won't fool us.

Sharing the Hope

Make good use of every opportunity you get, because these are bad days.
Ephesians 5:16

Back in the days of World War II people did not have television sets. They listened to the news of the war on the radio. Often the news was broadcast at dinner time, and children had to sit and eat quietly so their parents could hear the radio. A little girl grew very tired of always having the gloomy news broadcast at dinner time. She said to her brother, "I'll be so glad when the war is over. Then there won't be any more news broadcasts."

How disappointed she was when news broadcasts continued after the war! She learned that people always want to know what is going on in the world.

We know today that often the newspapers and television tell of bad news—fighting, crime, accidents. The good things that are happening seem to be overlooked. Perhaps that is why the apostle Paul said, "Make good use of every opportunity you get, because these are bad days." Christians have heard the *good* news that Jesus died for their sins. They know the peace and joy that he gives. This is the hope we can share. If someone in your family is feeling gloomy, perhaps you can do something especially kind and loving for him or her. If a friend seems to think everything is going wrong, maybe your kindness will give him or her hope again. Many opportunities come each day to share God's love. Watch for your chance today.

You're Needed at Worship

Speak to one another in the words of psalms, hymns, and sacred songs; sing hymns and psalms to the Lord, with praise in your hearts. *Ephesians 5:19*

Mrs. Logan stood in church one Sunday, singing the first hymn and planning her dinner. Just before church she had learned that her sister was coming to town to visit their mother who was sick in the hospital. Mrs. Logan wanted to make it a special dinner. Of course she was worried about her mother's illness, too. She sat down after the hymn, never thinking of the words she'd been singing. Her mind was on all her problems that morning.

The service continued and after a while the congregation was standing to say the Apostles' Creed. A beautiful clear voice came from behind Mrs. Logan: "I *believe* in God the Father Almighty. . . ." The voice was full of trust and hope as it spoke the familiar words so lovingly. Mrs. Logan's heart was lifted. Her mind was at worship. Her tense shoulders eased with God's peace. She longed to know who it was in back of her who spoke the familiar words in such a way that she was lifted out of her cares and strengthened. The service continued with Mrs. Logan participating with all her heart and mind. At the close of the service, as the congregation prepared to leave the church, she turned to see who was in back of her. A young girl with blond pigtails and two front teeth missing smiled at Mrs. Logan. The girl's father nodded good morning. *Just a little girl,* thought Mrs. Logan, *but what a difference she made in my morning.* Then Mrs. Logan whispered, "Thank you, God, for this dear child."

In our big Christian family, there is no one who isn't needed. Young, old, strong, weak—every kind of person is needed. God can use each of his people to strengthen the faith of others as happened in this story. He can use your words and singing, too.

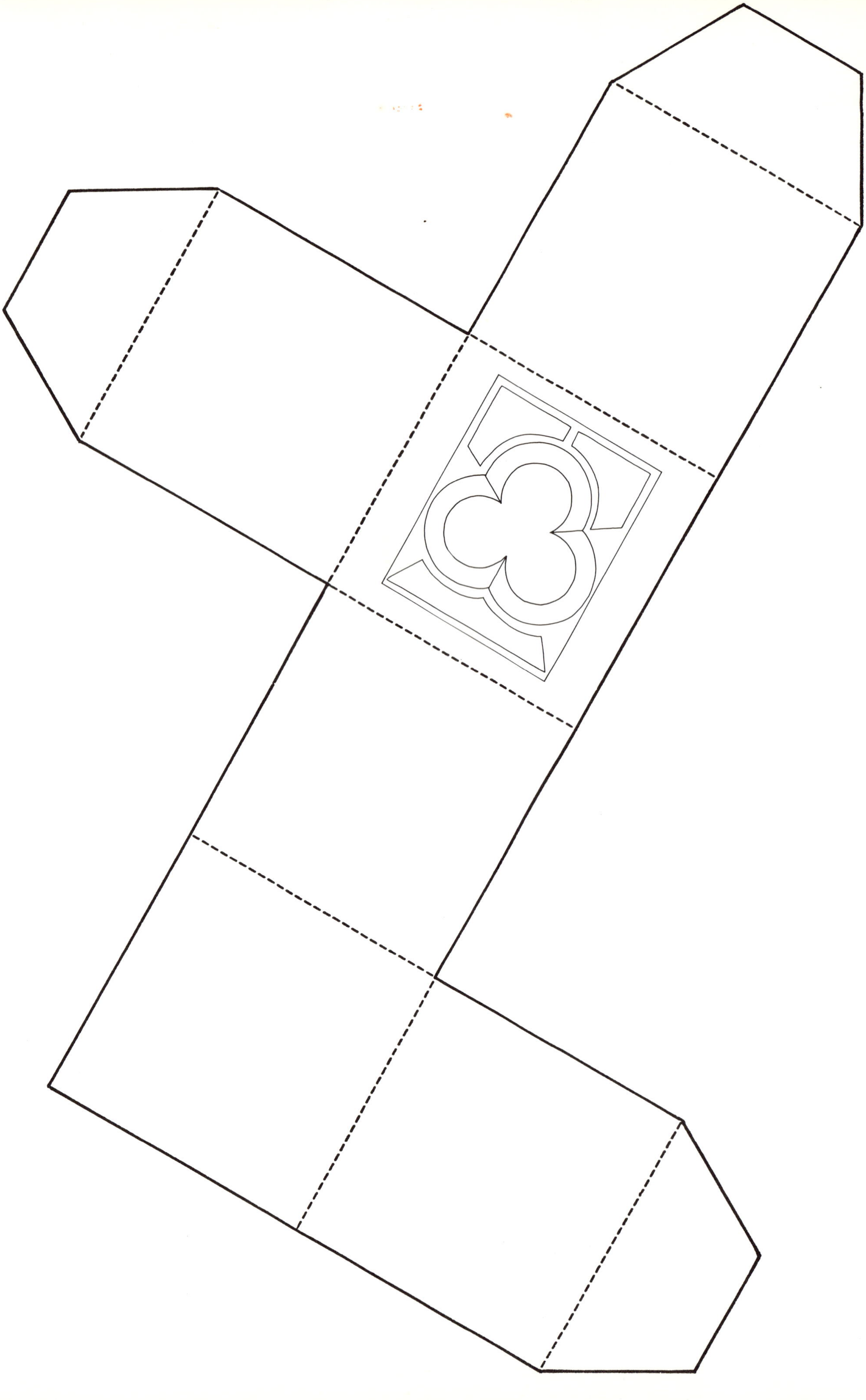